AN IDEAS INTO ACTION GUIDEBOOK

# Feedback That Works

## How to Build and Deliver Your Message

## IDEAS INTO ACTION GUIDEBOOKS

Aimed at managers and executives who are concerned with their own and others' development, each guidebook in this series gives specific advice on how to complete a developmental task or solve a leadership problem.

| | |
|---|---|
| LEAD CONTRIBUTOR | Sloan R. Weitzel |
| GUIDEBOOK ADVISORY GROUP | Victoria A. Guthrie |
| | Cynthia D. McCauley |
| | Russ S. Moxley |
| | |
| DIRECTOR OF PUBLICATIONS | Martin Wilcox |
| EDITOR | Peter Scisco |
| WRITER | Peggy Droz |
| DESIGN AND LAYOUT | Joanne Ferguson |
| CONTRIBUTING ARTIST | Laura J. Gibson |

CCL No. 405
ISBN No. 1-882197-58-5

CENTER FOR CREATIVE LEADERSHIP
POST OFFICE BOX 26300
GREENSBORO, NORTH CAROLINA 27438-6300
336-288-7210
WWW.CCL.ORG/PUBLICATIONS

AN IDEAS INTO ACTION GUIDEBOOK

# Feedback That Works

## How to Build and Deliver Your Message

Sloan R. Weitzel

Center for
Creative
Leadership

NORTH AMERICA  EUROPE  ASIA

www.ccl.org

# THE IDEAS INTO ACTION GUIDEBOOK SERIES

This series of guidebooks draws on the practical knowledge that the Center for Creative Leadership (CCL) has generated in the course of more than thirty years of research and educational activity conducted in partnership with hundreds of thousands of managers and executives. Much of this knowledge is shared – in a way that is distinct from the typical university department, professional association, or consultancy. CCL is not simply a collection of individual experts, although the individual credentials of its staff are impressive; rather it is a community, with its members holding certain principles in common and working together to understand and generate practical responses to today's leadership and organizational challenges.

The purpose of the series is to provide managers with specific advice on how to complete a developmental task or solve a leadership challenge. In doing that the series carries out CCL's mission to advance the understanding, practice, and development of leadership for the benefit of society worldwide. We think you will find the Ideas Into Action Guidebooks an important addition to your leadership toolkit.

# Table of Contents

## EXECUTIVE BRIEF

Whatever level you occupy in an organization, from line manager to senior executive to team leader, the skill of giving meaningful and effective feedback is an important component to helping other people develop and to getting the job done. Creating and delivering a specific message based on observed performance is key to effective feedback. Your feedback should enable the receiver to walk away understanding exactly what he or she did and what impact it had on you. When the result is this specific and this direct, there is a better chance that the person getting the feedback will be motivated to begin, continue, or stop behaviors that affect performance. This guidebook explains how to deliver effective feedback by showing how to build your message, when to deliver it, and how to communicate it. By using the methods and examples in this guidebook, your feedback becomes a tool for development – for others and for yourself.

# What Is Effective Feedback?

As a manager, you probably spend a good deal of time reviewing and measuring all kinds of information to understand the factors that affect your business. *What is my division's revenue versus expenses for the quarter and what is driving expenses up? What percentage of our quota has my division achieved year to date and what is left in the pipeline? What is our current production level and how can we increase capacity in the short term?* Determining specific quantifiable numbers and developing clear action plans to reach those numbers are integral components of a manager's job. Yet oftentimes the same managers who develop specific *what if* scenarios and examine business data with the intense rigor of a scientist use no such specifics or data when evaluating the company's most important capital: employee performance. Effective feedback requires that you use the same attention to detail that you employ when analyzing business information.

Creating and delivering a specific message based on observed performance is key to effective feedback. You may have told a fellow manager, a co-worker, or even your boss that he is a *good leader*, or that she *communicates well*, or that he *needs to be more strategic*. You may believe that such statements are helpful examples of feedback. But these statements only evaluate or interpret, they don't describe specific behavior so that a person can learn and develop by repeating or avoiding that behavior.

Effective feedback should enable the receiver to walk away understanding exactly what he or she did and what impact it had on you. When the result is this specific and this direct, there is a better chance that the person getting the feedback will be motivated to begin, continue, or stop behaviors that affect performance.

Think about statements you might have made to co-workers, bosses, or subordinates that concerned their performance. Then ask yourself: What did the person do that made you think he was a good leader? What did she say and how did she say it to make you think she communicates well? What did he do that made you conclude his thinking wasn't strategic enough?

In the pages that follow you'll learn how to answer questions like those as you develop your feedback skills. After you've read this guidebook, you will be able to:

- Give effective feedback to a boss, peer, or subordinate that accurately represents your thoughts without blame or judgment.
- Become more conscious of a person's actual behavior and the messages it sends.
- Increase your awareness of the emotional responses you have to the actions of others.
- Increase the likelihood that you will receive more effective feedback that you can use for your own development.

# Ten Common Mistakes in Giving Feedback

During many CCL programs, we ask managers and executives: "How many of you give good, consistent feedback to the people you work with?" Usually only one or two people raise their hands. Why so few? The reasons are varied: It's hard to do; I am afraid I will say something I will regret; people get emotional when they hear things they don't like; it might jeopardize my work relationships. All of these concerns are valid, but they all stem from common mistakes that people make when giving feedback:

1. *The feedback judges individuals, not actions.* Probably the number one mistake people make in giving feedback is putting it in judgmental terms. If you say to someone "You were too abrasive," or "You need to be a better team player," you send a strong message about what you think is "right" or "wrong" and that you've judged this person as falling short of expectations. Judgmental feedback puts people on the defensive. By the time the words are out of your mouth, your feedback recipient is already thinking "Who do you think you are calling me abrasive?" The energy spent defending themselves from your attack defeats any chance of a useful conversation.

2. *The feedback is too vague.* The second most common mistake made in giving feedback is the use of generalized, cliché catch phrases like "You are a good leader," "You did a great job on the presentation," or "You have a lot of common sense." The person hearing these words may be happy to get the compliment, but they won't have any idea of what exactly they did to

9

earn your praise. If you want to encourage someone to repeat productive behavior, you have to let them know what they did so they can keep doing it.

3. *The feedback speaks for others.* To say something like "Sheila said that you seem confused about your new assignment," or "People are telling me that they feel like you are micro-managing them," isn't effective feedback. At best the recipient will be perplexed by such statements and wonder where co-workers got such a notion or wonder just who is talking behind closed doors. At worst he or she may be embarrassed that such a comment came through you, a third party, and resent co-workers for making it in the first place. The person receiving the feedback is likely to become defensive and unable to hear your feedback.

4. *Negative feedback gets sandwiched between positive messages.* If you have to give negative feedback, it's tempting to first say some-thing positive, then deliver a negative statement, then soothe the situation with another positive message (a good-bad-good sandwich). Your intentions may be good, but you're mistaken if you think people hearing this kind of feedback get the right message. Instead, the recipient will soon figure out what you're doing, filter out the two positive ends, and focus on the nega-tive message in the middle.

5. *The feedback is exaggerated with generalities.* Another key mistake is using language like "always" or "never." Hearing these words, people naturally get defensive as they can remember plenty of times when they did not do what you claim they did.

6. *The feedback psychoanalyzes the motives behind behavior.* Telling someone that you know they are behaving a certain way be-

cause of an impending divorce, jealousy over a co-worker's advancement, or burnout is ineffective because what you think you know about someone's intents and motives is probably dead wrong. Feedback that goes to motive is likely to cause resentment on the part of the recipient.

7. *The feedback goes on too long.* Oftentimes when people give other people feedback, they don't know when to stop. They give advice, describe personal experiences, and try to solve the other person's problem. People receiving feedback need time to digest and assimilate the information they have just received.

8. *The feedback contains an implied threat.* Telling someone her job is in jeopardy ("Do you want to be successful in this organization?") doesn't reinforce good behavior or illustrate bad behavior. It only creates animosity.

9. *The feedback uses inappropriate humor.* If giving feedback is uncomfortable to you, or if you sometimes speak before thinking, you might use sarcasm as a substitute for feedback. But saying "good afternoon" to a colleague who is ten minutes late for a morning meeting doesn't tell that person how that behavior affected you or provide reasons to change that behavior.

10. *The feedback is a question, not a statement.* Phrasing feedback as a question ("Do you think you can pay closer attention during our next meeting?") is too indirect to be effective. It may also be interpreted as sarcastic, to which the recipient may respond defensively, or rhetorical, to which the recipient may respond with indifference.

# Developing Effective Feedback Skills

You can avoid common feedback mistakes by learning how to communicate important information about performance to subordinates, peers, or superiors in a way that helps them hear what you are saying and helps them identify ways in which they can improve. During the course of giving feedback to tens of thousands of people over many years, CCL has developed a feedback technique we call SBI, shorthand for Situation-Behavior-Impact. Using this technique, which CCL teaches to thousands of managers every year, you can deliver feedback that replaces personal attack, incorrect judgments, vague statements, and third-party slights with direct and objective comments on a person's actions. Hearing this kind of feedback, the recipient can more easily see what actions he or she can take to continue and improve performance or to change behavior that is ineffective or even an obstacle to performance.

The SBI technique is effective because it's simple. When giving feedback you describe the situation, you describe the behavior you observed, and you explain the impact that the behavior had on you. Simple, direct, and effective—if you learn the three steps and practice them regularly. In the following pages, we will show you how to use each component of the SBI approach.

## Capture the Situation

The first step in giving effective feedback is to capture and clarify the specific situation in which the behavior occurred. If you say "On Tuesday, in the break room with Carol and Fred," rather than "A couple days ago at the office with some people," you avoid the vague comments and exaggerations that torpedo so many feedback opportunities. Describing the location and time of a behavior creates context for your feedback recipients, helping them remember clearly their thinking and behavior at the time.

Remember, capturing the situation is only the start of your feedback session. Here are a few examples of how you might successfully describe a situation when giving feedback:

- "Yesterday morning, while we were inspecting the plant . . ."
- "Last Monday, after lunch, while we were walking with Cindy to the meeting . . ."
- "Today, first thing this morning, when you and I were talking at the coffee machine . . ."
- "This past Friday night, at the cocktail party for the new marketing manager, when Karl was explaining his new job description . . ."

Specificity is important when recalling a situation. The more specifics and details you can use in bringing the situation to mind, the clearer your message will be.

### Describe the Behavior

Describing behavior is the second step to giving effective feedback. It's also the most crucial step and the one most often omitted—probably because behavior can be difficult to identify and describe. The most common mistake in giving feedback happens when judgments are communicated using adjectives that describe a person but not a person's actions. That kind of feedback is ineffective because it doesn't give the receiver information about what behavior to stop or to continue in order to improve performance. Consider the phrases below:

- He was rude during the meeting.
- She was engaged during the small-group discussion.
- She seemed bored at her team's presentation.
- He seemed pleased with the report his employees presented.

These phrases describe an observer's *impression* or *interpretation* of a behavior. Now look at the following list of actions an observer might witness that would lead to those impressions and interpretations.

- He spoke at the same time another person was speaking. *(Rude)*
- She leaned forward in her chair, wrote notes after other people spoke, and then said her thoughts to the group, repeating some of the things that other people said. *(Engaged)*
- She yawned, rolled her eyes, and looked out the window. *(Bored)*
- He smiled and nodded his head. *(Pleased)*

The phrases in this list use verbs to describe a person's actions. The focus is on the actual behavior, not on a judgment as to what the behavior might mean. If you remember to use verbs when describing behavior, you avoid the mistake of judging behavior. By focusing on the action, not the impression, you can communicate clear facts that a person can understand and act on.

In order to become more adept at identifying behavior and, in turn, be better able to effectively communicate what you have seen to the feedback recipient, you have to capture not only *what* people do but *how* they do it. The new CEO who stands before her company and says "I'm excited to be your new president" will appear insincere if she has no expression on her face, speaks in a flat voice, and uses no hand gestures. So when giving people feedback using

### Difficult Behaviors

To understand how difficult identifying behaviors can be, look over the following list. Put a check next to the phrases that describe behaviors:

\_\_\_\_ Overconfident
\_\_\_\_ Very aggressive
\_\_\_\_ Needs to be less tactical and more strategic
\_\_\_\_ Arrogant
\_\_\_\_ Analytical and extremely logical in her approach
\_\_\_\_ Good team player who cares about the people in his department
\_\_\_\_ Extremely productive
\_\_\_\_ Excellent all-around manager
\_\_\_\_ Decisive

If you didn't check any, then you're right on track. None of the phrases in the list describes a behavior. Behaviors are actions that people take. In contrast, the above list includes *adjectives* that describe the person—not the person's actions.

SBI, it is not only important to capture *what* is said or done but *how* it is said and done. You can capture the *how* by paying attention to three things: body language, tone of voice and speaking manner, and word choice.

*Body language* is nonverbal communication and can include facial expressions, eye movement, body posture, and hand gestures. For example:

*Jim was becoming increasingly irritated with Alice during their meeting. Alice frequently shook her foot, shifted in her seat numer-*

*ous times, tapped her pen on the table repeatedly, and nodded her head at people as they passed by her cubicle while he was talking.*

Although Alice never spoke, she sent loud and clear messages through her body language. Jim can begin to give Alice effective feedback by saying something like the following:

*"Alice, during our meeting yesterday in your cubicle I noticed that you looked at your watch several times during a fifteen-minute period. You tapped your pencil loudly on the table and shifted from side to side in your seat. You also nodded your head at people as they passed by your cubicle while I was speaking."*

Jim has communicated the *situation* and many clear instances of *behavior* to Alice. His approach will help Alice understand the *impact* of her behavior (the final step of giving effective feedback).

*Tone of voice and speaking manner* relates to the pitch of a person's voice, the speed and volume at which the person speaks, and the pauses used when speaking. (Broadcasters, especially sportscasters and news anchors, are masters of this.) Voice mannerisms can be hard to notice and describe for the purpose of giving effective feedback, but can be useful behavioral cues. For example:

*Jason is introducing a new product idea to a group of his peers. During his presentation he pauses on at least six different occasions, halting in midsentence. After these pauses, his voice slows down considerably. He speaks in a low monotone. When people ask him questions, he suddenly speaks very fast. He ends his talk saying "Thank you, thank you very much" in a tone that is louder than he has used throughout the whole speech.*

Some of the impressions that Jason might have created for you may include *uncertain, nervous, hesitant, not a good presenter.* But to say just that to him doesn't help him develop. Effective feedback would include a description of Jason's speaking manner. You would talk about *how* he presented the material—the pauses, the tone and volume of his voice—as well as his body language:

> *"Jason, during your presentation yesterday you stopped several times and spoke so low that it was difficult for me to hear you. Then, toward the end of your presentation, when people asked questions, you spoke faster and your voice got louder. The way you presented made me feel like you weren't well prepared or that you didn't care much about your presentation, and the way you spoke faster at the end made me feel like you were in a rush to get out of the room."*

A person's *choice of words* often can be the least important component of behavior. Nevertheless, capturing the specific language a person uses during a specific situation can help you give effective feedback.

> *During a face-to-face team meeting with a small development group, Bob loses his temper when he learns that Fred will miss a deadline. Bob calls Fred a loser in front of the entire group. When the meeting breaks up, the team members quietly file out without speaking to one another.*

If the content of a person's message has an impact on you and you want to give effective feedback, write down the speaker's words so you can remember exactly what was said:

> *"Bob, during the team meeting this morning you called Fred a 'loser' in front of the whole group. I was really uncomfortable that you singled out one person and used that kind of insult. After hearing that, I felt that we weren't a team at all."*

**Points of Delivery**

- When you approach someone to offer feedback, use a phrase such as "May I share an observation with you?" This open approach, in which you ask permission, can ease anxiety and sets the scene for a conversation, not a confrontation.
- To create more openness around the notion of feedback, ask for permission to give feedback, say something positive, ask if the person understands what behavior you're talking about, then stop talking and walk away. This positive approach can ease the fear many people have when they hear the word "feedback."
- Acknowledge the uneasiness or discomfort you may feel when giving a person feedback. Say something like "As I'm telling you this, I'm aware of how uncomfortable I am." A simple acknowledgment honors your experience and can minimize the perceived threat of the feedback experience from the receiver's perspective.

### Deliver the Impact

The final step in giving effective feedback is to relay the *impact* that the other person's behavior had on you. The impact you want to communicate is not how you think a person's behavior might affect the organization, co-workers, a program, clients, a product, or any other third party. The impact you want to focus on and communicate is *your* reaction to a behavior. There are two directions you can take when sharing the impact of a person's behavior.

1. You can evaluate or make a judgment about the person's behavior: *"I thought you showed interest when you asked for the group's opinions."* This tactic is the most common, but it is also the less effective of the two because the person getting the feedback can argue with your interpretation of the behavior.

2. You can acknowledge the emotional effect the person's behavior had on you. *"When you told me in the meeting that my concerns about product deadlines were 'overblown,' I felt belittled."* This approach can be more effective than the first because it truly is your reaction to someone's behavior, a reaction that only you experience. The person hearing your feedback can't easily dismiss your personal experience, and so is more likely to hear what you've said.

   By communicating the personal impact a behavior has had on you, you are sharing a point of view and asking the other person to view that behavior from your perspective. That kind of sharing helps to build trust, which in turn can lead to even more effective feedback as communication is improved. If you have difficulty finding the right word to describe the impact a behavior has had on you, take a look at our list on page 26 for help.

   To develop your effectiveness in carrying out the impact stage of giving feedback, practice putting your feedback in the form of *"When you did (behavior), I felt (impact)"* or *"When you said (behavior), I was (impact)."* Here are some examples of how you might use this form when giving feedback. (The examples illustrate the entire SBI form, with the impact statement underlined.)

   Peer feedback. *Sophie, this morning in the hallway you asked for my opinion about decisions to launch our new product. You also* *often ask me to join the group at lunch. <u>That makes me feel included, part of the team.</u>*

**Subordinate feedback.** *Matt, in the meeting with the new vice-president yesterday, you kept your voice at an even tone, even when she questioned your numbers. You held out your hand with your palm up several times. <u>I felt really at ease with your delivery.</u>*

**Boss feedback.** *Karen, you have not commented once about the field reports I have completed. <u>I feel slighted.</u>*

# Maintaining the Message

Now you know that to successfully give effective feedback you must recount a specific situation, describe the precise behavior, and explain what impact the behavior had on you. But even when you know the proper form, there are pitfalls to avoid when you deliver effective feedback, traps that can detract from your message and weaken the developmental opportunity feedback provides. CCL's experience in training managers how to give effective feedback has highlighted ten key traps to watch out for.

1. If you back out of the feedback you give, the receiver will lose your message. *"You interrupted me, which made me feel angry, but the more I think about it, it was pretty hectic at the time . . ."*

2. If you pull in your own experiences, you take ownership away from the feedback receiver. *"I remember when I did that . . ."*

3. If you pull in your own vulnerability, you presume to know what the receiver is experiencing or thinking. *"I used to have the same problem . . ."*

4. If you cushion your feedback, you can put the receiver on the defensive and he or she will be less open to your message. *"You're not going to like hearing this . . ."*

5. If you label your feedback, you can create undue anxiety and the receiver may not hear your entire message. *"I have some negative feedback to give you . . ."*

6. If you give advice with your feedback, the receiver may think you have a personal agenda. *"Let me tell you what you need to do to have a successful team meeting."*

7. If you label behavior as a problem, you put the receiver on the defensive and your message may not be heard. *"You have a problem getting your expense reports in on time."*

8. If you don't use words that precisely communicate your message, or are insensitive to the language that you use, you can cause unnecessary emotional reactions. *"You were a real windbag in that meeting this morning."*

9. If you judge the person, not the behavior, the person hearing your feedback will likely become defensive and resentful. *"You were disruptive today."*

10. If you delay in giving feedback, your memory of the event might not be clear enough to be specific, and the receiver might wonder why the conversation didn't occur sooner. *"Last month when we were attending the regional trade show . . ."*

# Putting It All Together

Review the situation, behavior, and impact steps that build effective feedback and practice those steps at every opportunity. You don't have to wait for an actual feedback situation to arise to review your skills. For example, the next time you attend a trade show and hear a compelling presentation, think about what you are experiencing that makes the presentation so valuable. Observe the speaker and take note of the situation, the speaker's behavior, and the impact that behavior is having on you. Is the speaker using hand gestures? What about tone of voice? What kinds of facial expressions is the speaker making? Are the speaker's words appropriate for the audience and the subject?

After you've practiced at a distance like this, it can be helpful to practice with a willing partner, preferably someone at work. You can address a simple situation with a simple impact, but use an instance that really takes place (an imaginary situation won't help much). State the facts (situation and behavior), then give your response (impact).

Take time to reflect on your feedback efforts. Ask yourself, "Why did I pay attention to this particular behavior? What does this say about me?" Perhaps you've observed behaviors that you want to develop in yourself or behaviors you want to drop or guard against. Reflection also gives you time to understand the true nature of the impact the behavior had on you. Ask yourself, "How did I feel when she talked to me in that tone of voice?" or "What emotional response did I have when he shook my hand and said my reports showed good research and attention to detail?" Reflection will help you become more concise and focused in delivering your feedback message, and help you avoid traps that weaken your message.

As you become more familiar with the approach and more comfortable with the delivery, your feedback skills will become more and more effective. The people you work with—your boss, colleagues, and subordinates—will benefit from the effort you put toward helping them develop. You in turn will benefit from developing a useful skill that not only helps to raise the productivity of all the people around you but also bolsters your personal leadership skills.

# The Dozen Do's and Dont's of Effective Feedback

## Do

1. Be specific when recalling the situation.
2. Be specific when describing the behavior.
3. Acknowledge the impact of the behavior on *you*.
4. Judge the behavior.
5. Pay attention to body language.
6. Use verbatim quotes.
7. Re-create the behavior, if appropriate.
8. Give feedback in a timely manner.
9. Give your feedback, then stop talking.
10. Say "I felt" or "I was" to frame your impact statement.
11. Focus on a single message.
12. Be sensitive to the emotional impact of your feedback.

## Don't

1. Assume.
2. Be vague.
3. Use accusations.
4. Judge the person.
5. Pass along vague feedback from others.
6. Give advice unless asked.
7. Psychoanalyze.
8. Qualify your feedback by backing out of the description.
9. Use examples from your own experience.
10. Generalize with words like "always" or "never."
11. Label your feedback as positive or negative.
12. Sandwich your feedback messages with words like "but."

# Words with Impact

Getting just the right word to express the impact a behavior has on you is important. The right word can help keep your feedback from being vague or misconstrued. Finding the right word, however, isn't always easy. To help you put impact into words that you can deliver as effective feedback, we compiled this short list of descriptive impact words.

| | | | |
|---|---|---|---|
| Ambivalent | Frightened | Miserable | Skeptical |
| Angry | Frustrated | Nervous | Spiteful |
| Annoyed | Glad | Odd | Startled |
| Astounded | Good | Outraged | Stupid |
| Betrayed | Gratified | Overwhelmed | Sure |
| Bored | Happy | Peaceful | Sympathetic |
| Burdened | Helpful | Persecuted | Tempted |
| Calm | Helpless | Petrified | Tense |
| Captivated | Honored | Pleasant | Tentative |
| Challenged | Hurt | Pleased | Terrible |
| Diminished | Ignored | Pressured | Terrified |
| Disturbed | Impressed | Proud | Threatened |
| Divided | Infuriated | Refreshed | Tired |
| Ecstatic | Inspired | Rejected | Troubled |
| Electrified | Intimidated | Relaxed | Uneasy |
| Empty | Isolated | Relieved | Unsettled |
| Excited | Jealous | Restless | Vehement |
| Exhausted | Kind | Rewarded | Vital |
| Fearful | Left Out | Sad | Vulnerable |
| Flustered | Lonely | Satisfied | Welcome |
| Foolish | Low | Scared | Wonderful |
| Frantic | Mad | Shocked | Worried |

# Suggested Readings

Brutus, S., & Manoogian, S. (1997). The art of feedback. *Leadership in Action, 17*(3), 8-10. Greensboro, NC: Center for Creative Leadership.

Buron, R. J., & McDonald-Mann, D. (1999). *Giving feedback to subordinates.* Greensboro, NC: Center for Creative Leadership.

Dorn, R. C. (1982). Performance problems: Taking action. *Issues & Observations, 2*(3), 6-7. Greensboro, NC: Center for Creative Leadership.

Fleenor, J. W., & Prince, J. M. (1997). *Using 360-degree feedback in organizations: An annotated bibliography.* Greensboro, NC: Center for Creative Leadership.

Goleman, D. (1998). *Working with emotional intelligence.* New York: Bantam Books.

Kirkland, K., & Manoogian, S. (1998). *Ongoing feedback: How to get it, how to use it.* Greensboro, NC: Center for Creative Leadership.

Laborde, G. (1987). *Influencing with integrity.* Palo Alto, CA: Syntony Publishing.

McCauley, C. D., Moxley, R. S., & Van Velsor, E. (Eds.). (1998). *The Center for Creative Leadership handbook of leadership development.* San Francisco: Jossey-Bass and Center for Creative Leadership.

Roush, P. E. (1992). The Myers-Briggs Type Indicator, subordinate feedback, and perceptions of leadership effectiveness. In K. E. Clark, M. B. Clark, & D. P. Campbell (Eds.), *Impact of leadership* (pp. 529-544). Greensboro, NC: Center for Creative Leadership.

Stone, D., Patton, B., & Heen, S. (1999). *Difficult conversations.* New York: Viking Press.

Van Velsor, E., Leslie, J. B., & Fleenor, J. W. (1997). *Choosing 360: A guide to evaluating multi-rater feedback instruments for management development.* Greensboro, NC: Center for Creative Leadership.

# Background

The advice given in this guidebook is backed by CCL's research and educational experience, which has over the years demonstrated the value of (1) assessment for development and (2) systemic development.

Assessment for development has been a focus of CCL since its beginning in 1970. At that time, standard business practice was to evaluate employee performance but not to share the results of those evaluations with the employees themselves. When CCL developed its Leadership Development Program (LDP)®, that notion was set aside and replaced by the then radical idea of sharing evaluation information with the people being evaluated. That sharing was, and still is, a feedback-intensive experience.

CCL understood from the start that developing the capacity to lead was not something that could be accomplished by a single event. CCL research and experience helped that understanding evolve to a recognition that leadership must be developed by means of a continual and systemic process, and that an essential component of this process is ongoing feedback.

# Key Point Summary

Oftentimes managers who develop specific "what if" scenarios and examine business data with the intense rigor of a scientist use no such specifics or data when evaluating the company's most important capital: employee performance. Information about performance, delivered in a way that is clear, nonjudgmental, and specific, helps all employees identify ways in which they can improve. Effective feedback requires that you use the same attention to detail that you employ when analyzing business information to the development of your leadership skills.

During the course of giving feedback to tens of thousands of people over many years, CCL has developed a feedback technique we call SBI, shorthand for Situation-Behavior-Impact. Using this technique, you can deliver feedback that can help the recipient more easily see what actions he or she can take to continue and improve performance or to change behavior that is ineffective or even an obstacle to performance.

The SBI technique can be described by its three components. The first step in giving effective feedback is to capture and clarify the specific *situation* in which the behavior occurred. Describing *behavior* is the second step to giving effective feedback. The final step is to relay the *impact* that the other person's behavior had on you.

As you practice this technique and put it into action, there are some pitfalls of which you should be aware. For example, don't back out of the feedback with "second thoughts." Don't cushion your feedback with such phrases as "You aren't going to want to hear this . . . " as it tends to put your audience on the defensive.

Review the situation, behavior, and impact steps that build effective feedback and practice those steps at every opportunity. Take time to reflect on your feedback efforts. As you become more familiar with the approach and more comfortable with the delivery, your feedback skills will become more and more effective, and the people around you will benefit from your improved leadership in this area.

# Related Publications

## ONGOING FEEDBACK

Information on your performance from co-workers and colleagues is essential if you are to develop new managerial skills and hone current ones. This guidebook provides a method of ensuring that you receive a steady flow of this feedback. (Stock No. 400)

## GIVING FEEDBACK TO SUBORDINATES

Providing specific information about performance is key to developing the people who report to you. This guidebook tells you how to give your subordinates effective feedback so they can work more effectively, develop new skills, and grow professionally. (Stock No. 403)

## FEEDBACK THAT WORKS

Providing feedback to others about their performance is a key developmental experience. But not all feedback is effective in making the best use of that experience. This guidebook demonstrates how to make the feedback you give more effective so that others can benefit from your message. (Stock No. 405)

Purchase our **FEEDBACK GUIDEBOOK PACKAGE** and receive the above three titles at a significant savings. See below for ordering information.

## OTHER CCL PRESS RELATED PUBLICATIONS

Choosing 360: A Guide to Evaluating Multi-rater Feedback Instruments for Management Development (Stock No. 334)

Enhancing 360-degree Feedback for Senior Executives (Stock No. 160)

Feedback to Managers: A Review and Comparison of Multi-rater Instruments for Management Development (Stock No. 178)

Maximizing the Value of 360-degree Feedback: A Process for Successful Individual and Organizational Development (Stock No. 295)

Should 360-degree Feedback Be Used Only for Developmental Purposes? (Stock No. 335)

Using 360-degree Feedback in Organizations: An Annotated Bibliography (Stock No. 338)

# Ordering Information

FOR MORE INFORMATION, TO ORDER OTHER IDEAS INTO ACTION GUIDEBOOKS, OR TO FIND OUT ABOUT BULK-ORDER DISCOUNTS, PLEASE CONTACT US BY PHONE AT 336-545-2810 OR VISIT OUR ONLINE BOOKSTORE AT WWW.CCL.ORG/GUIDEBOOKS. PREPAYMENT IS REQUIRED FOR ALL ORDERS UNDER $100.